CAREER SUCCESS SECRETS

CAREER SUCCESS SECRETS

Thrive in Your Professional Life

B. VINCENT

QuantumQuill Press

CONTENTS

CHAPTER 1

Introduction

This book is about how to thrive in the professional realm, and yes, take advantage and benefits from what you are already doing. You will find strategies to help you have goals reaching professional effects and how to maintain and maintain your motivation and is particularly practical for you to learn the techniques to overcome certain work-related challenges. So, from now on, try to start enjoying Monday morning as much as Friday night. The goal of this book is simple, to allow you to achieve professional satisfaction according to your aspirations and needs, and in case you are not yet where you want, this guide should also help you take the first steps towards such achievement. Oh, don't feel lonely, you are not the only one in that situation. In writing this book, we use statistics from several sources, which we report regularly. Statistics are informative and can help you understand if the work problems you face are similar in other places or if they reflect operational culture or beliefs, and the attitudes you have are not common.

We cannot avoid the question of a job because we spend a lot of time working. In other words, there is much more to life than work, but at the same time we have to work, and with luck, it can be a pleasure. The belief that working through the week in horror has the reward of leisure on the weekend is a belief that resigns us to live in a way that we do not like. So how do you feel about your access to obscene work? A growing number of people are beginning to think differently, and in any context, they seek ways to find meaning and happiness in the job they have chosen as a priority or not. They understand that work does not have to be something heavy and exhausting to endure to be successful.

CHAPTER 2

Building a Strong Foundation for Success

Is your growth strategy helping or hindering your personal and professional growth? Do not mistake activity with accomplishment. One of the greatest leadership and career success secrets is actively focusing on self-improvement. Career professionals with positive personal principles ahead of self-indulgence practices foster an enriching personal integrity that are the building blocks to a successful career life. Professionals live by professional principles and possess a durable character because their practices are rooted in prudence, fortitude, temperance, and justice. Sound judgment does not always track with age, but when it does, patience grows. Professionals who have achieved significant personal growth are evident in their harmonious justice, self-restraint, and humility as expanded in professional self-improvement ideas and other growth strategies.

Success in a career begins with the right foundation - building such will enable the harvest of time-tested and proven career success secrets. Knowing where you want to go in your professional life, embracing a set of professional principles, making the right career choices, and establishing practical, possible, and achievable career plans and goals are the basic ingredients. Discover your professional growth areas and build your journey to self-improvement guided by these career success secrets.

2.1. Setting Clear Goals

Too many of us get confounded and discouraged because we tend to have unattainable targets or goals that aren't precisely expressed. In order to achieve career success, neither should be the case. Thinking about your career is about what you want. It's about your future. What will satisfy you at work? What legacy do you want to leave behind? If you do not establish this for yourself now, you will be working towards fulfilling somebody else's dream. That is not your ideal scenario, is it? If you don't establish your ideal career, you will suffer in the unfortunate event that you have lost your job, and the message might get muddled. Set well-defined accomplishments and work towards them. Clear figures, as well as how you will measure them, may often set off an internal fire that encourages you.

If you want career success, you must first establish what that looks like and set clear goals. What do you want to accomplish, and by when? Remember to be realistic. Establishing clear and attainable targets is the most powerful motivator you can use to drive yourself to accomplish those things that lead to career success. But in order to know what you are aiming for, you also need a highly defined strategy. Based on your career objectives, what steps are you most likely to follow? Then, what do these next steps consist of? Who specifically do you need to reach out to? How? Set in writing what in each phase you are going to do specifically.

2.2. Developing a Growth Mindset

If you have to use the word "yet", use it. Focus on your personal development and you will be amazed by the results. Try to grow every day. Help others do the same. Anyone can attain a growth mindset in four phases: awareness, action, commitment, and dedication. This is a continuous process, as anyone who ever achieved success will agree. Success is guaranteed. While in the fixed mindset the person paved the way, entering deep, narrow thoughts and experiencing rapid anxiety, in the growth mindset one is keenly aware of organization, discipline, and patience. With these in mind, you will be excited, making progress regularly, and will enjoy the journey.

The growth mindset maintains that individuals can change their intelligence and become smarter and display improved abilities, which is contradictory to the theory of fixed intelligence. Executives such as Growth Coach Founder Rick Davis and Google Senior Vice President Paul Otellini suggest implementing some of the following tips so that you can keep your eyes open for them. See what you can learn from them. Your relatives, teachers, bosses, and colleagues have all managed to prevent you from putting your championship skills to work now. Ignore them, be whomever you want to be and go for it!

Developing a growth mindset; Achieving your professional goals; Super effective time management. We have already established the importance of lifelong learning in today's rapidly changing world. The foundations of lifelong learning are curiosity and a growth mindset. Below are a few tips that can help you maintain a growth mindset. Your mindset might play the biggest role in your success. Two extreme ideas are supporters of the fixed mindset, which believes that we cannot change three basic elements: our intelligence, our talents, and our abilities. On the other hand, the growth mindset brings optimism and wants to develop and be creative.

2.3. Building a Professional Network

Scientists have pointed out that during communication, people evaluate the speaker not only according to the speaker's speech, but also according to the listener's reaction, suggesting that extroverts are usually seen as good communicators than those who cannot adapt to the situation. People pay more attention to the behavior of the listener than the speaker's speech. This means that one must adhere to the principle of "give to get" on networking. The target of this rule is to give as much as possible and to make others feel that they have taken the initiative to provide the necessary help. In this way, a good relationship can be built and resources will be provided when needed.

In today's world, professional social connections can significantly help you get to the top in your career. The famous saying on networking: "Your network is your net worth" has proven to be true when high-efficiency professional networking is carried out. It is not at all about the number of people you know. It is about the range of people you know and how valuable they are to you as your career moves forward. Whether it's a professional network or personal network, the key to success lies largely in what both parties can contribute. For those at a relatively high level today, professional circles are much more important because of the resources they can share.

CHAPTER 3

Mastering Essential Skills

Believe it or not, it is not because of technical knowledge. I saw good architects, too clever troublemakers, become parts of quarrels in their firms simply because they did not know how to dialogue with stakeholders, did not know how to negotiate with managers or vendors, customers. This is where we are going to be successful or not. It is at this point that the star will play or will flop. That is why their perception of value is relative and can, most of the time, range from very high to zero. Since there are some soft skills that professionals must master to be successful in their corporate career, which are the most important? Key competences are essential skills. All the famous lists of mega professions always announce that they are looking for professionals who have the competencies to collaborate, who work well on good teams. Professionals are not on the lookout just for what they know how to do, but also for "how they are", which competencies they have. It is beside the point to be excellent 'sole super must act in a balanced way. In the midst of so many related professional actions, which are consistent with the strategic planning of their collaborator, the right word is to act in favor of the strategic planning of their collaborator-in-chief, always seek to add.

Career success secrets: Thrive in your professional life. 3. Mastering essential skills. There are some skills that you just need to have in the corporate world. Not all these capabilities are necessarily job-related. On the contrary, when you hear that someone is doing well or that they are a star in their profession, it is not entirely because they are capable. They owe that brightness to behavioral and soft skills. When people look inside a company, that is, they look at a mass, they will see what differentiates the mass tends to hide from view. The more someone draws attention, the more diffusion they have, the more they attract followers, usually on the outside, right? However, what guarantees the star's high performance, in a technical aspect, in time? It is right to say that what anchors an individual like that in time are their behavioral standards, their soft skills, their intrapersonal skills, such as initiative, assertiveness, leadership, sympathy, capacity for dialogue, negotiation, sales, influence, problem-solving, resilience.

3.1. Effective Communication

Another detail about communication is being a listener. How good are you at listening to others' issues? How do you act during a conversation? Do you pay attention or do you keep standing defensive, hoping to find a new visitor for your own zoo? Listening is complex and usually not appreciated by other people. At the business level, decision making and problem solving depend on others' opinions and capabilities to come up with ideas for new work dynamics. Sharpening your listening skills can widen your own perspectives.

Communicating your ideas is a must if you want to thrive in your professional life. The challenge is not only in showing your ideas to others, but in doing so clearly and assertively enough for people who are listening to catch your message and understand it. Word art is essential for this. Talking is an art, yet sometimes it is not enough to be good at it. To illustrate that, let's make an association with presenters who are good at talking but lack the ability to present. You know the type of person who is good at filling the time of the presentation with beautiful wording, but once finished, you are tired, your head is spinning, and you do not even know what that person was talking about, since no message was conveyed. It is no use to have the most beautiful wording if your idea did not make sense or was not understood. Therefore, you have to make an enormous effort to evolve and be able to communicate effectively, with messages simple enough for others to understand and complex enough to allow you to make yourself understood properly.

If you check any list of the most wanted skills by employers, you will find that interpersonal skills are always in the top ten. The same happens with interpersonal competences, which are always present in the top ten.

3.2. Time Management and Prioritization

There are some moments where we may have to change our approach to work, but always have clear goals in mind and perseverance. At the end of the day, it always pays off. While it requires one form of energy or another, it leads us to success and happiness. That said, the reverse can also be a fact. If we do not have a clear path to follow, perseverance can lead us to situations of greater stress and despair. Be patient with yourself in these situations and be ready with the tools to help us. Get organized. Do not be concerned with your position in relation to others or even with luck at this time. Have full focus on personal development since the competition is essentially with yourself. Evaluate everything that will happen and have clear periodic deadlines to overtake yourself. Deciding to overcome our work each day that goes beyond our limits can deceive the competitors, especially when these targets are high.

Another important factor in determining an individual's success is time management and prioritization. Successful professionals know how to manage their time effectively and, as such, focus on doing similar work that, when grouped, offers them the best effect. They know what their most important work is and execute it. They know the exact tasks to allocate to improve themselves or increase their organization's advantage over the competition. They manage their time so well that, come rain or shine, they complete their work on time. Therefore, always care for your time. Once it is lost, it cannot be recovered.

3.3. Problem-Solving and Decision Making

What one views as an "issue" is a fundamental dilemma identifying business operability. This difficulty may also be a thing that presents extraordinary positive impacts. The criteria for solving problems may be reasonably limited in various ways. We appear to think of moving through the challenge process naturally when we listen to or study the difficulties of other persons have settled. Studies show that the use of our analytical system based on fact in response to the difficulties of famous persons of yore ends in revolutionary and requisite culmination. In a more structured and practical approach, difficulties may also be approached involving models that come back. When we learn and carry out what we know, the demon of submitting to identities ensures that we choose strategically. A small proportion of men is recognized as trouble solution solvers by doing and by developing identifiable skills for challenge resolution.

We live in a time wherein the world is changing significantly all the time. There is a variety of solutions for every issue and the consumer world is rapidly changing. In any job, a person first solves troubling problems or finds innovative, revised products or procedures. Also, the issue of deciding what works best comes up as a subject in a plethora of problems. There are a variety of factors in determining what sorts of issues occur, but the most common ones are working form, knowledge, means, time, and management. The capability to process a collection of various sorts of issues at work that are prevalent, key, and will probably continue to help every individual life.

3.4. Adaptability and Resilience

Resilience is understood as the ability to overcome and grow after experiencing adversity, proving to wrap around this challenge with a constructive and positive learning experience, providing the individual who experiences it the ability to foster ever stronger levels of reconstruction with their own history. Resilience is an extremely important factor of adaptability and is one trait that the vast majority of hiring managers are eager to find in their future employees. Many businesses know that when changing the directions or needs of the company, they will need employees to change their processes and procedures too, and this attribute can greatly facilitate these changes. In professional life, resilience can be the determining foundation that dictates the resilience of an employee. Likewise, emotional intelligence, problem solving and adaptability work in a reciprocal setting in which adaptability and resilience are also based on emotional intelligence and a solid problem-solving approach.

Adaptability describes the ability of an organization, person or system to adjust its actions in order to habituate more efficiently to a new context. It is an attribute that separates successful workers from the less successful ones. There are many possible factors affecting job and career success, and some of the most associated attributes include adaptability, resilience and positive attitudes. Whereas current research on actual development of adaptability attributes oriented towards an empirical reality still slightly differs, this review article highlights recent conceptual clarifications, elaborations and derivations and suggests some future challenges based on several influential models of adaptability that share common attributes. These common attributes can be exploited to enhance adaptability both in scientific research and in practical life.

You aspire to change careers, get a new job or advance in your current job. No matter what your aspirations are, you need some tools to stand out and demonstrate the exceptional worker you are. Here we will explore many key and useful concepts for achieving the success you deserve in your professional life in the most practical way possible.

CHAPTER 4

Advancing Your Career

Make sure to put your plan into action, and concentrate on being identified by the right individuals, particularly those who head initiatives that fall within your professional aspirations. With the drive to progress, the chances of improving your career will explode, and the company will gain a recognized role across departments.

It is also essential to understand the trajectory you need to establish to remain engaged and dedicated to the company. If you determine it can't be performed and your goals are relevant to your professional path, you should have the determination and dedication to take action. This may indicate discovering another division, jumping to another business, or considering other career possibilities.

It is very important to discuss your goals with your supervisor and determine how you can work together to make them happen. In today's organization, it's imperative to discuss career direction with supervisors and to understand the advice, support, and opportunities they will make available to you. Candid interaction with your supervisor will allow you to gather insight and appreciate their reasoning.

3. Create an action plan and get to work. Whether your end goal is a more senior position in your department, moving to another part of your company, or to another company, choose the steps you need to take to make your desired transition happen.

2. Understand your opportunities within your company. What is the next position you would apply for if it were open today? Which other options would you consider?

1. Make a list of your top career goals. What is the next step in your career? Concentrating on becoming more knowledgeable, for example, of the specifics of your job, or broadening your expertise by getting business training can raise your profile and make you more valuable to your employer.

We all have projects and assignments to work on, weekly team and all-hands meetings to attend, lunch breaks and emails to catch up on. But amid all this hustle, it's easy to forget that we are ultimately responsible for our own careers, and have complete control over our own destinies. To get out of the day-to-day and plan where our professional journeys should take us next, we need to make sure we carve out that time, adjusting our actions in the micro and macro to make those goals happen and ensure that no opportunities pass us by.

4.1. Continuous Learning and Skill Development

Learning feeds your mind and the more educated you are, the more your brain has to prevent from dementia. It's that simple and, if it helps, count learning as going to the gym for your head. But it's not just about keeping cognitive decline at bay. When you learn, you get better at what you do and become more effective. It's impossible to get ahead if you're not good at what you do, isn't it? It doesn't stop there. You are a unique individual. Your knowledge and experience are different from the next person's. So when you learn a new skill or gain new knowledge, you differentiate yourself from the competition. And that helps when it's time for a salary negotiation, a job change or even a promotion.

You may want to think of your career as a concrete climb: go to school, get a degree, skill up a little and boom—at the top. But it doesn't work that way. Not in an age where skills have a shelf life of fewer than five years. Not in an age where, according to the World Economic Forum Future of Jobs Report, "some skills can remain in demand—or even experience growth—amid radically shifting industry requirements." So, a crucial career success secret in this day and age is to keep learning and developing your skills throughout their careers, even when not job-hunting.

4.2. Seeking Mentorship and Guidance

Mentorship: They come in all shapes and sizes and have a wide variety of qualities. They are the cheerleaders from childhood to the mediocre teacher that inspired revolutionary thinking. Mentors are the secret weapon in any career. You're the owner of a circle of friends that are the foundation of what defines you. They have a beautiful mosaic of the direction you are headed, but a mentor has even more. Just as with our mothers and best friends, mentors are emotionally invested in our actions and decisions. In any given work situation, they can help us confront what we've always known or interrupt the thought pattern that until now has only been a rumor. Clean group think with a low level of echo chamber will always bring you back to the place that says, "this is important and I'm good enough". In picking a mentor, safety and trustworthiness ride shotgun with a diverse range of expertise in the industry. At times, people just start the job, get busy, and use up their mentor's time because they can get it for free. Understand that all the signs above could mean someone could make excellent mentor material, but don't fall asleep after someone becomes your mentor. This isn't a coffee shop. They are molding you, not smothering you.

The DIY (Do-It-Yourself) culture is great for learning and exploring new ideas, but for other life tasks, it's good to invite the help of a professional. Kitchen remodels and bathroom fixes are at the top of the list of home repairs that homeowners should leave to the experts. We know our limitations in the arena of mold, mildew, and rusty pipes. One aspect of life that doesn't have to suffer from water damage is your career. Recognizing that we could all use a little guidance from time to time, we've compiled a list of professionals that no career should go without.

4.3. Taking on Leadership Roles

In this section you will learn how to put in some extra effort at work, volunteer to lead the next project. Being a leader exposes you to benefits beyond mentors trips and higher wages. You also develop better understandings of how businesses operate. More specifically, you see firsthand what or who drives organizational success. For those trying to pivot to the role, the key is to construct a relevant story that demonstrates how you think and why you are a good fit for a leadership role. Leaders are the decision-makers in the enterprise working on actionable strategies to achieve goal completion. Given what they do, you're going to have an easier time implying that you understand both the people and processes in place. A legitimate understanding helps you select the right networking sessions and beef up looks on your résumé as well as in your cover letter.

Full-time jobs offer guaranteed hours, a lot of room for growth and leadership opportunities. Whether you're a shift manager or an assistant manager, you have plenty of opportunities to put your leadership skills to use and amplify them. Leadership on your résumé could mark a major turning point in your career. The role isn't just helpful in symbolic ways like boosting leadership skills and showing off a new job title. It also has tremendous potential for boosting your income. Management and leadership roles regularly rank as "in-demand" job opps, and this category offers several strong potential positions that you can only get through experience as a manager or assistant manager. These include: Care home manager, Business travel consultant, Benefits manager, Hospitality and leisure and management export coordinator. The best option for you really depends on your passion and natural skills. You can also ask your manager about the Many Hands program to learn to coordinate, plan and direct almost every aspect of your work party.

4.4. Navigating Organizational Politics

Politicking at the workplace is about talking ill of Ms. Jones who is being thrust to lead a big project the company won. It is about pulling down expectations toward a new leadership and acting negatively towards your organization. It is about circumventing all authority levels with the aim of acquiring power to achieve personal interests at the expense of your team. It is about sacrificing professionalism and honesty in the name of protection. Forming and operating effectively in alliance networks is one of the ways, appreciating the values, locations, and fundamental premises that store relationships and knowledge that ultimately lead to power within the organizational setting. Forming alliances with supportive networks are unconventional and under-recognized because they are made up of busy people in the organization. Not implementing is one key cause of project failure regardless of size, scale, and industry.

Think of your workplace as a big party. And as in all parties, there are parties within the party, groups within the group. Organizational politics is about being able to move and fit in these groups effectively, without changing your identity. But mind you, influencing power of any form should not be used to work against your organization, colleagues, and customers or to personally benefit. For sure, you must befriend influential people, both directly and indirectly. To do this, you need to constitute additional understanding at different levels.